How to Use This Book

The **Teaching Versions** of *Elements of Reading* help you guide students to become fluent readers. Because fluency is not an isolated skill but is closely linked to word knowledge and comprehension, each **Teaching Version** contains the following types of teacher support:

- **Fluency teaching suggestions** to help students become proficient in reading with expression (prosody).

- **Word knowledge teaching suggestions** to build students' proficiency in reading words and understanding their structure and meanings. The word knowledge suggestions address high-frequency words, decoding skills, structural analysis skills, and knowledge of word meanings.

- **Sentence comprehension questions** to help students develop literal comprehension at the sentence level.

- **Text comprehension questions** to help students develop inferential comprehension. Additional comprehension questions are provided in the **Teacher's Lesson Folder**.

After students complete the repeated reading activity outlined on page 1.12 of the **Teacher's Lesson Folder**, use the reduced **Student Book** pages and teaching suggestions in this **Teaching Version** to provide explicit page-by-page instruction.

Your Body Up Close

■ **Fluency Focus**

Expression Using stress to convey meaning
Punctuation Observing junctures indicated by commas
Text Format Reading chapter titles

■ **Word Knowledge Focus**

Decoding Words with multiple syllables
High-Frequency Words (Boldface words appear in each book of the theme.)

a, about, all, and, are, as, at, **back**, big, body, can, carry, close, cold, come, cut, day, do, **don't**, down, each, eat, even, **every**, eye, far, feel, feet, food, from, get, grow, has, have, **head**, hear, help, hot, how, if, in, into, is, it, keep, let, light, little, **live**, look, made, make, more, most, move, much, need, new, not, now, of, old, on, one, or, other, out, over, part, people, place, really, red, round, see, so, some, **something**, tell, than, that, the, their, them, then, there, these, they, this, time, to, too, under, up, use, when, white, with, work, you, your

■ **Sentence Comprehension Focus**

Comprehending stated details

■ **Text Comprehension Focus**

Identifying main ideas and details

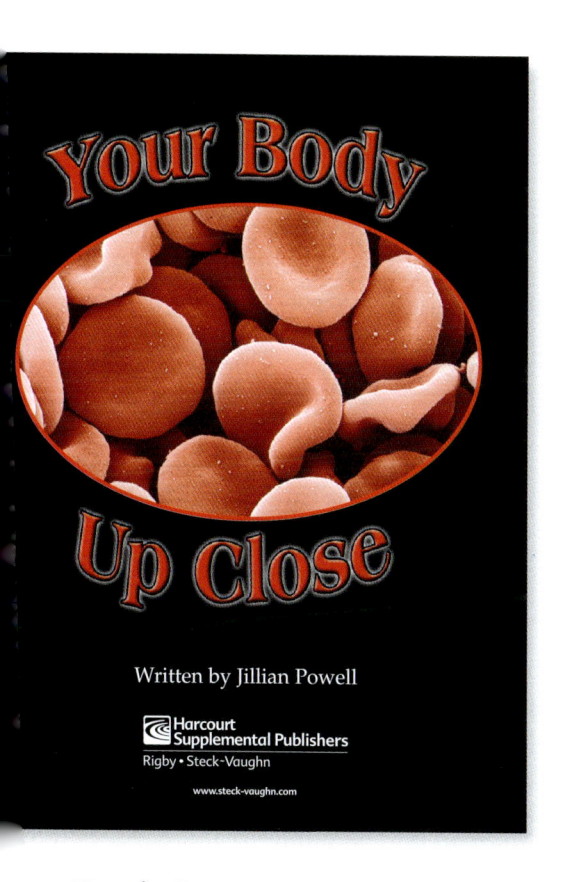

Getting Started

To begin, invite a volunteer to read the title page aloud.

Book Summary

This nonfiction book begins by introducing cells. It then explores the kinds of cells found in the skin, mouth, eyes, ears, hair, and nails, and describes the function of each. The book concludes by discussing how microscopes help doctors to study these tiny things.

Explain the purpose of a table of contents—to list the page number on which each chapter of the book begins. Point out that when we read books aloud, we usually do not read the table of contents.

Contents

Introduction	3
Chapter 1 **Your Skin**	4
Chapter 2 **Your Mouth**	8
Chapter 3 **Your Eyes and Ears**	12
Chapter 4 **Your Hair and Nails**	16
Chapter 5 **Looking at Cells**	20
Glossary	23
Index	24

Introduction

Your body is made from millions of tiny parts called cells. Cells are so tiny that you need something to help you see them. You can use a microscope to see the cells in your body. A microscope makes cells look much, much bigger.

▼ Your body is made from millions of cells.

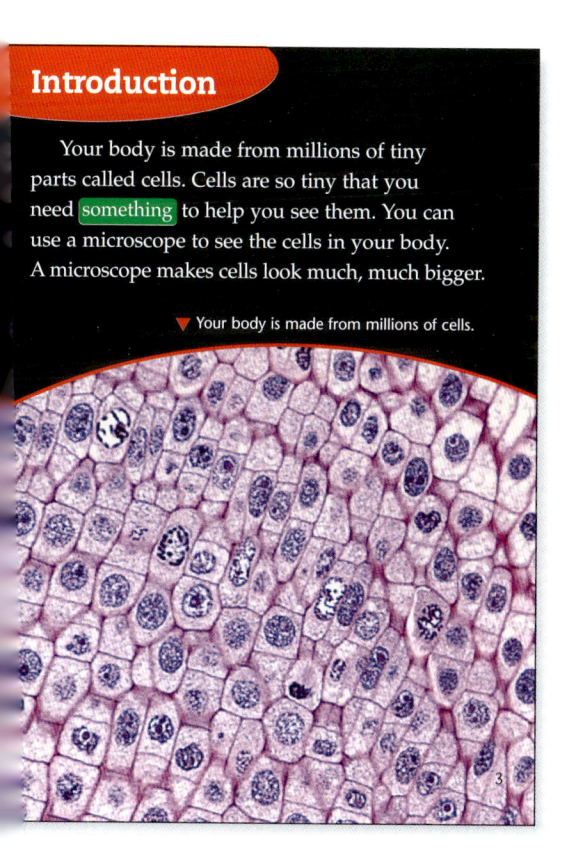

■ Sentence Comprehension

Ask *What are cells?* (tiny parts of the body)

■ Fluency

Suggest that reading nonfiction aloud should sound like we are explaining something. When we explain something, we stress some words to make sure listeners understand key ideas. Model reading the first sentence, using the boldface words below as a guide:

Your **body** is made from **millions** of **tiny parts** called **cells**.

Ask students to identify the words you stressed.

■ Word Knowledge

Invite a student to write the theme high-frequency words (*back*, *don't*, *every*, *head*, *live*, and *something*) on the board. Ask which word from the list appears on the page.

■ Fluency

Read the page without pausing after the chapter title and again with a pause. Ask students which reading they think is correct. Guide students to understand that pausing after the chapter title gives the listener a clue about what will follow.

Read the paragraph aloud, emphasizing the words "old," "new," "dead," and "every day." Ask students to identify the words you stressed and the places you paused.

Have students scan the page to find sentences with commas. Invite volunteers to read the sentences aloud to demonstrate pausing briefly at a comma.

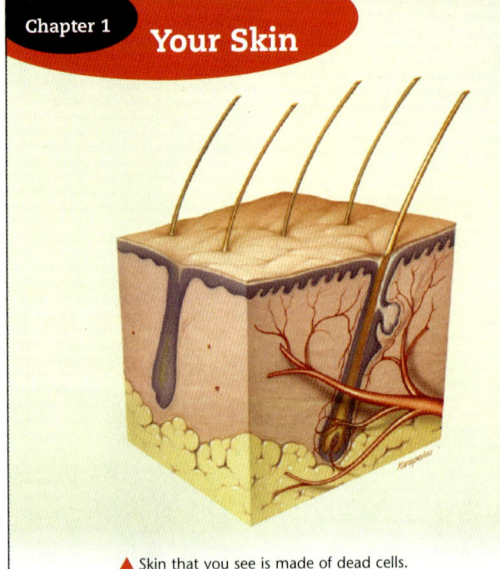

Chapter 1 **Your Skin**

▲ Skin that you see is made of dead cells.

Your skin is made of old and new cells. The top of your skin is made of old, dead cells. Every day, you lose lots and lots of these cells. New skin cells grow under the old cells.

4

■ Sentence Comprehension

Ask *What is skin made of?* (old and new cells)

▼ Sweat comes out of the skin through pores.

Your skin helps to keep you cool. Skin has tiny holes called pores. Every time you get hot, drops of sweat come out of each pore. The sweat dries on your skin. It helps you feel cool.

■ Sentence Comprehension

Ask *What are pores?* (tiny holes in the skin)

■ Fluency

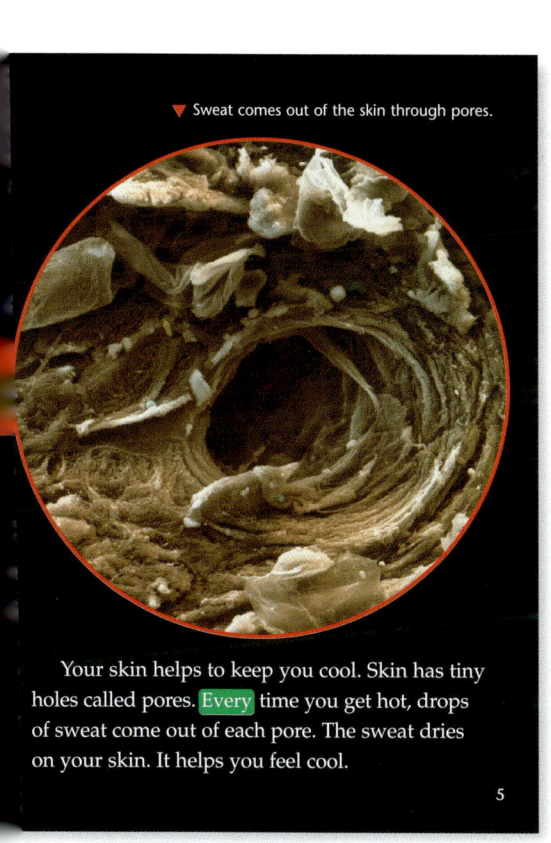

Point out the comma after the introductory phrase "Every time you get hot" in the third sentence. Have students read the sentence together.

■ Word Knowledge

Have students read the list of theme high-frequency words aloud with you. Then ask students which word appears on pages 4–5.

■ **Fluency**

Point out the comma in the first sentence and the group of words that precedes it. Point out that a fluent reader pauses after other groups of words and sentences, even when no comma follows the words. Read the first sentence aloud, pausing at the places marked by slashes below:

If you feel cold / or something scares you, / you get goosebumps / on your skin.

Lead students in an echo reading of the sentence. Then have students identify the places to pause in the next sentence. (You get goosebumps / when tiny muscles under your skin / pull the roots of your hairs.)

▲ Goosebumps form when you are cold or scared.

If you feel cold or something scares you, you get goosebumps on your skin. You get goosebumps when tiny muscles under your skin pull the roots of your hairs. Each hair then stands up.

■ **Sentence Comprehension**

Ask *When do people get goosebumps?* (when tiny muscles under your skin pull the roots of your hairs)

▼ Bumpy skin is good for gripping things.

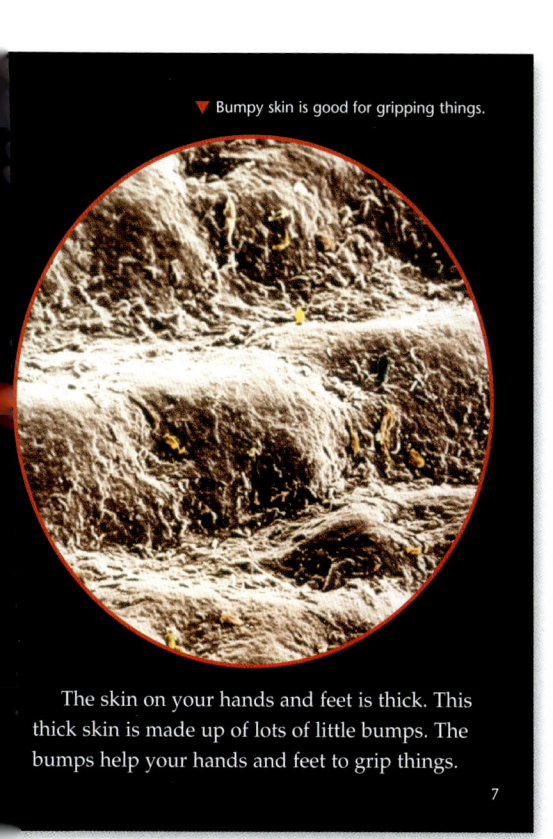

The skin on your hands and feet is thick. This thick skin is made up of lots of little bumps. The bumps help your hands and feet to grip things.

7

■ **Sentence Comprehension**

Ask *What do the bumps on your hands and feet help to do?* (grip things)

■ **Word Knowledge**

Direct students' attention to the list of theme high-frequency words on the board. Ask students which of the words appears on page 6.

Explain that a syllable is a word or word part with one vowel sound. Ask students how many syllables are in the word "muscles" on page 6. Invite students to name other two-syllable words on pages 6–7 ("something," "goose-bumps," "tiny," "under," "bumpy," "gripping," "little").

7

■ **Fluency**

Invite a volunteer to read the chapter title aloud. Ask students what they should do after a chapter title (pause).

Direct students' attention to the comma in the first sentence. Explain that "too" is an important word because it signals a comparison. Ask what is being compared (bumps on the tongue to bumps on hands and feet).

Then ask what the commas in the third sentence do (separate things in a series).

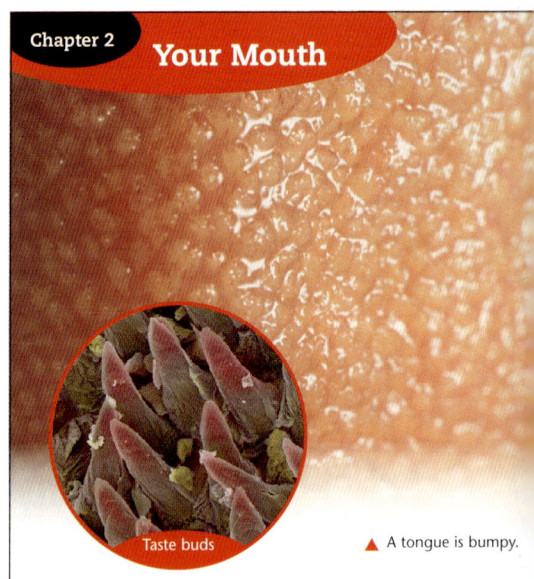

Chapter 2 — Your Mouth

Taste buds

▲ A tongue is bumpy.

Your tongue has lots of tiny bumps, too. Some of these bumps have cells called taste buds. Taste buds tell you if something is sweet, sour, or salty. Most of your taste buds are on the sides and back of your tongue.

8

■ **Sentence Comprehension**

Ask *What do taste buds do?* (They tell you if something is sweet, sour, or salty.)

▼ Saliva helps you swallow food.

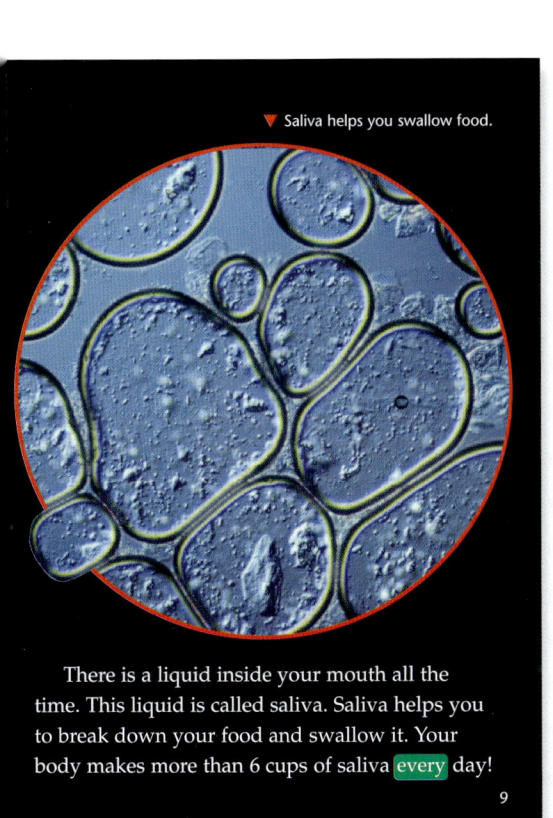

There is a liquid inside your mouth all the time. This liquid is called saliva. Saliva helps you to break down your food and swallow it. Your body makes more than 6 cups of saliva every day!

■ Sentence Comprehension

Ask *What is saliva?* (a liquid in your mouth)

■ Fluency

Read aloud the first sentence word by word. Then read it in phrases ("There is a liquid / inside your mouth / all the time"). Have students discuss the difference between reading word by word and in phrases.

■ Word Knowledge

Refer students to the list of theme high-frequency words on the board. Ask students which of the words appear on pages 8–9.

Ask students which words in the first sentence on page 9 have two syllables ("liquid," "inside"). Ask which word in the third sentence has three syllables ("saliva").

■ **Fluency**

Invite volunteers to read the page aloud. Encourage each reader to read in phrases, stress important words, and pause at punctuation marks. Point out that not all readers will stress the same words. Make comments that compliment expressive and clear readings.

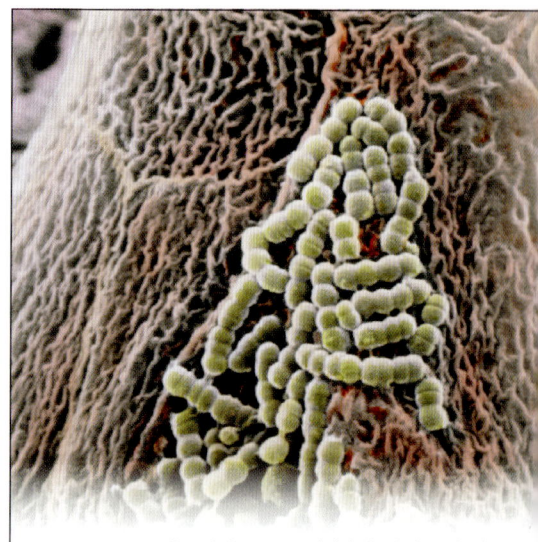

▲ Bacteria in your mouth help break down food.

Lots of tiny things live on your body. They are called bacteria. Some bacteria live in your mouth. Most of the bacteria in your mouth keep you healthy. They help to break down the food that you eat.

■ **Sentence Comprehension**

Ask *What are bacteria?* (tiny things that live on the body)

▼ Some bacteria stick to your teeth.

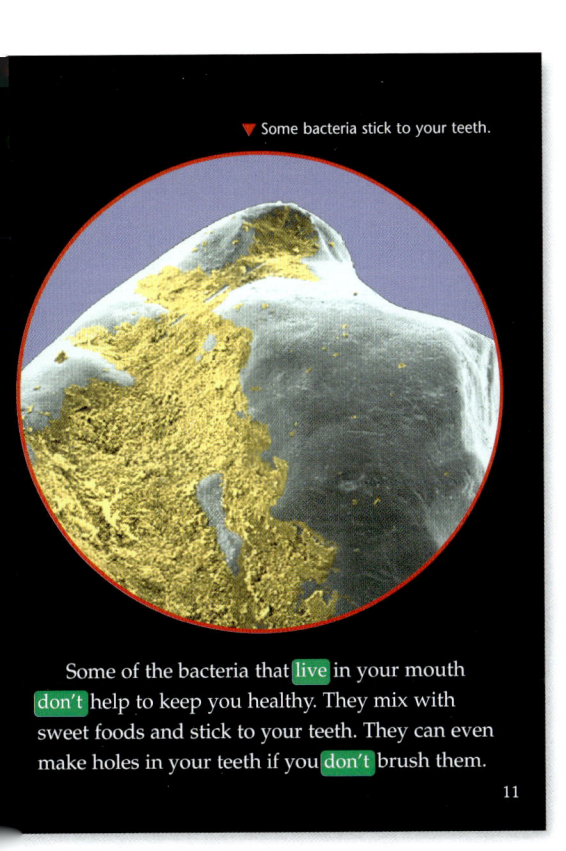

Some of the bacteria that `live` in your mouth `don't` help to keep you healthy. They mix with sweet foods and stick to your teeth. They can even make holes in your teeth if you `don't` brush them.

■ **Word Knowledge**

Have students find the theme high-frequency word *live* on pages 10 and 11 and *don't* on page 11.

Ask students to find a four-syllable word on the pages ("bacteria"). Invite students to name other four- syllable words they can think of.

■ **Sentence Comprehension**

Ask *What sometimes happens when bad bacteria mix with sweet foods?* (They stick to the teeth and can make holes in them.)

■ Fluency

Invite a volunteer to read the chapter title. Ask students what this chapter will be about. Invite a volunteer to read the page aloud. Remind the volunteer to pause after reading the chapter title, read in phrases, and stress important words. Then have students identify stressed words.

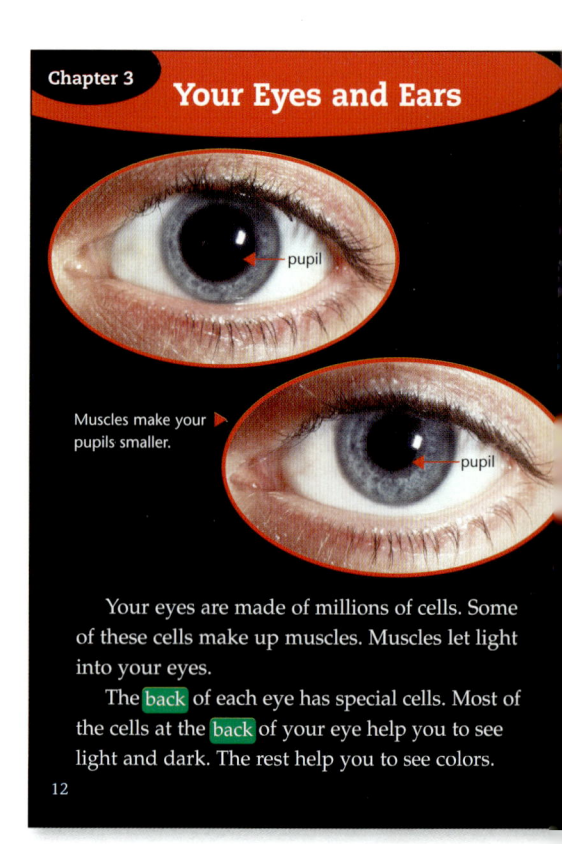

Chapter 3

Your Eyes and Ears

pupil

Muscles make your pupils smaller.

pupil

Your eyes are made of millions of cells. Some of these cells make up muscles. Muscles let light into your eyes.

The `back` of each eye has special cells. Most of the cells at the `back` of your eye help you to see light and dark. The rest help you to see colors.

12

■ Sentence Comprehension

Ask *What do muscles do for the eyes?* (They let light into them.)

▼ Eyelashes keep the eye safe.

Eyelashes are the hairs on your eyelids. Each of your eyes has about 200 eyelashes. They keep dust and dirt out of your eyes.

13

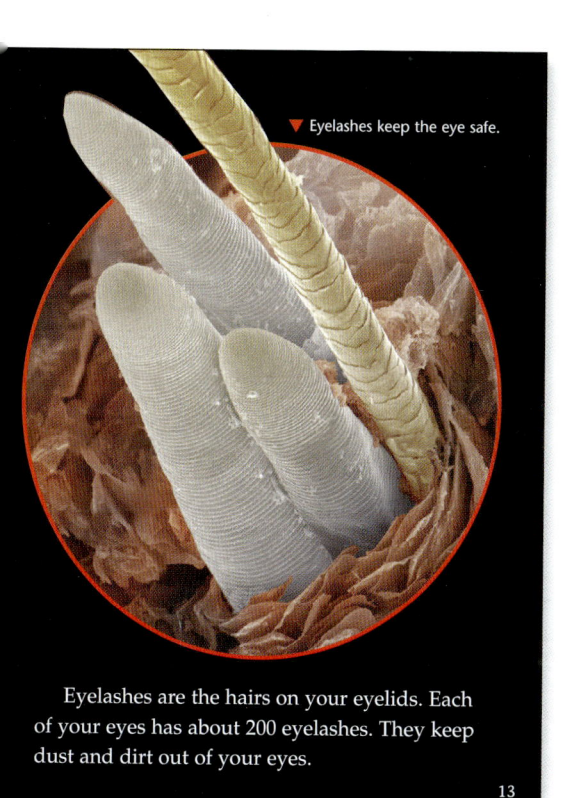

■ Sentence Comprehension

Ask *What do eyelashes do?* (They keep dust and dirt out of the eyes.)

■ Fluency

Write the page 13 text on the board and have students underline words they think should be stressed.

■ Word Knowledge

Have students find the theme high-frequency word *back* on page 12.

Have students find the words "muscles," "millions," "eyelashes," and "eyelids" on pages 12–13 and ask how many syllables are in each word.

■ **Fluency**

Write the first sentence on the board. Discuss with students where to mark the sentence for pauses and which words to stress. Use the slashes and boldface words below as a guide:

Inside each / of your **ears** / are **millions** / of **cells**.

Have students read the sentence together and then the rest of the page.

▲ Some ear cells carry sound.

Inside each of your ears are millions of cells. Special cells in each ear help you to hear. How do they do this? They carry sounds to your brain.

14

■ **Sentence Comprehension**

Ask   *What do cells in the ear do?* (They help people to hear.)

▼ Some ear cells help you keep your balance.

Other cells in your ear help you keep your balance. These cells are inside tiny tubes filled with liquid. As you move your head, the liquid moves. The cells move, too. The cells tell your brain to help you keep your balance.

15

■ Sentence Comprehension

Ask *Why are the cells inside the ears important?* (They help people keep their balance.)

■ Fluency

Point out the comma after the introductory phrase "As you move your head" in the third sentence. Ask students what the comma signals (pause).

Then point out the comma before "too" in the next sentence. Remind students that "too" is an important word because it signals a comparison.

Have students read the page chorally. Make sure they pause at the commas.

■ Word Knowledge

Have students find the theme high-frequency word on page 15.

Ask students to name words on the page that have two syllables ("balance," "inside," "tiny," "liquid").

15

■ **Fluency**

Call on a volunteer to read the page in a way that shows how *not* to read it. Then have the volunteer read it with pauses, phrasing, and stressed words.

■ **Word Knowledge**

Ask students how many syllables are in the words "million," "body," "tiny," and "curly" (two).

Chapter 4: Your Hair and Nails

Curly hair ▶

Straight ▶ hair

You have about 5 million hairs on your head and body. These hairs grow out of tiny tubes in your skin. Straight hairs are round, and curly hairs are flat.

16

■ **Sentence Comprehension**

Ask *How many hairs are on your head and body?* (about 5 million)

▼ Hair is made from dead cells.

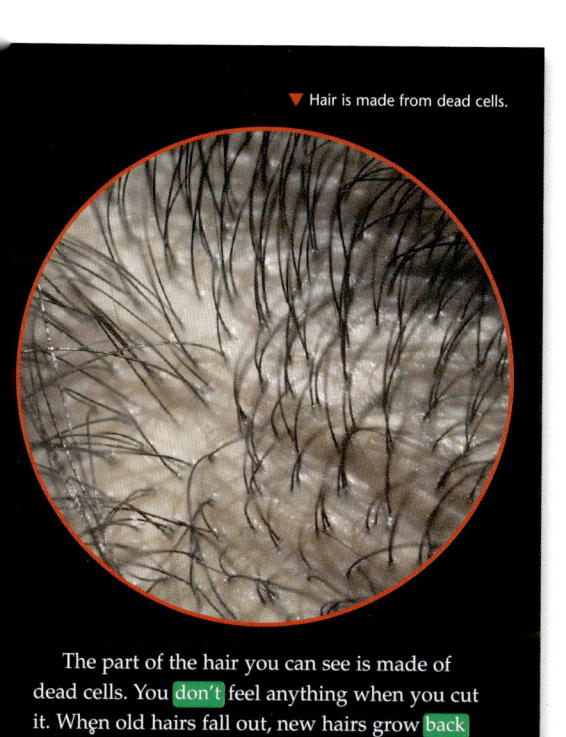

The part of the hair you can see is made of dead cells. You don't feel anything when you cut it. When old hairs fall out, new hairs grow back in their place.

■ Sentence Comprehension

Ask *Why doesn't it hurt when you cut your hair?* (The part of the hair that you cut is made of dead cells.)

■ Fluency

Lead students in an echo reading of the page.

■ Word Knowledge

Have students read aloud the list of theme high-frequency words on the board. Ask students which words are on pages 16–17.

■ Word Knowledge

Have students find the theme high-frequency word *head* on the page.

Ask students to find a two-syllable word on this page ("body," "fingers").

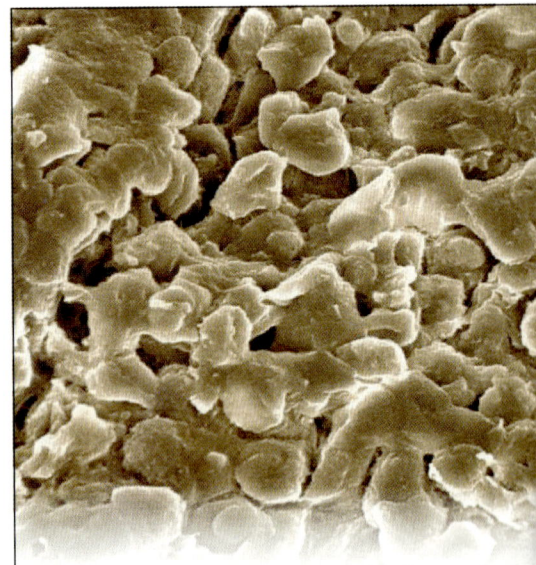

▲ Nail cells are very tough.

The hairs on your head and body are made of cells. So are your nails. Nails keep your fingers and toes safe from knocks and bumps. Nail cells are strong and tough.

■ Sentence Comprehension

Ask   *What do nail cells do?* (They keep fingers and toes safe from knocks and bumps.)

▼ When you cut your nails, you are cutting off dead cells.

Your nails grow over the tips of your fingers and toes. The part of the nail that you can see is made from dead cells.

■ Fluency

Discuss with students places to pause slightly and words to stress. Have volunteers read aloud to demonstrate their ideas.

■ Sentence Comprehension

Ask *Why doesn't it hurt when you cut your nails?* (That part of the nail is made from dead cells.)

Chapter 5 — Looking at Cells

Microscopes help people to understand how their body works. Doctors use microscopes to see if cells are healthy or not. Doctors look at blood cells under a microscope.

▼ Doctors can tell if cells are healthy.

■ **Fluency**

Invite a volunteer to read the page aloud. Make sure the volunteer pauses after reading the chapter title. Have students tell which words the volunteer stressed.

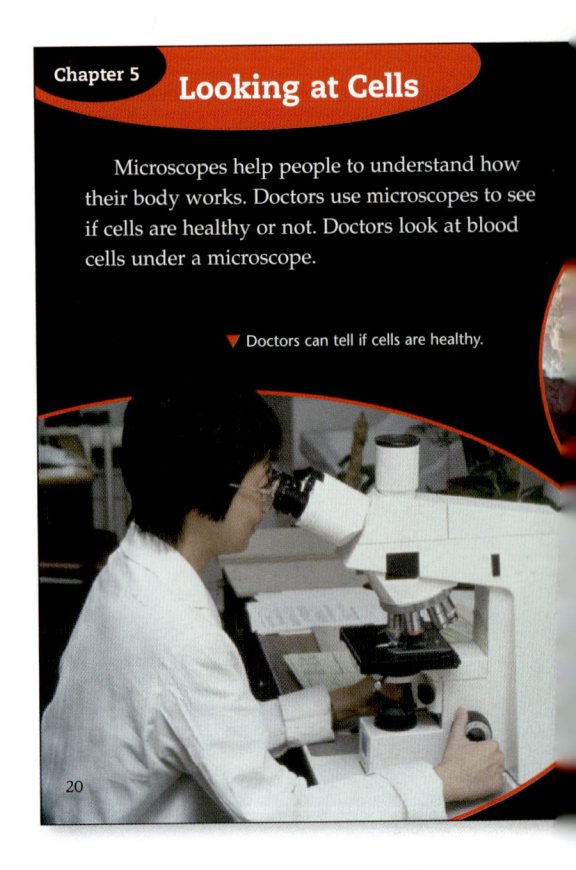

■ **Sentence Comprehension**

Ask   *What do microscopes help people do?* (understand how their body works)

▼ White blood cells fight germs.

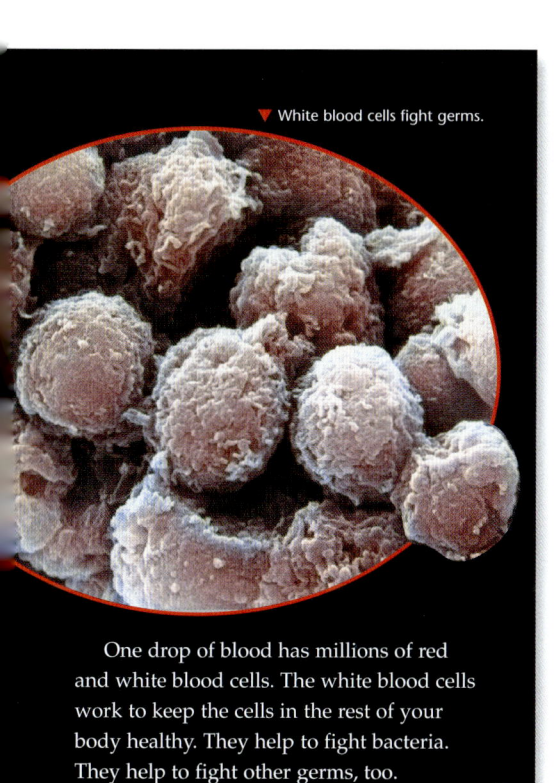

One drop of blood has millions of red and white blood cells. The white blood cells work to keep the cells in the rest of your body healthy. They help to fight bacteria. They help to fight other germs, too.

21

■ Sentence Comprehension

Ask *How many cells are in one drop of blood?* (millions)

■ Fluency

Read the last sentence without a pause before the word "too." Ask students whether you read the sentence well and elicit a good reading (one with a pause before "too") from volunteers.

■ Word Knowledge

Say the following words aloud: "microscopes," "understand," "healthy," "bacteria." Ask students how many syllables are in each word (three, three, two, four).

■ **Fluency**

Lead the class in an echo reading of the page. Make sure students follow your phrasing and word stress.

▲ Computers help people use the biggest microscopes.

Some microscopes are far too big to fit in your classroom. With these microscopes, you can make things look millions of times bigger than they really are. Now that's up close!

■ **Sentence Comprehension**

Ask *What can very powerful microscopes do?* (make things millions of times bigger)

Glossary

bacteria	tiny, one-celled living things
balance	a steady, even position of the body
cells	the tiny units of a living thing
germs	tiny living things that can make people sick
microscope	a tool that makes things look bigger
muscles	groups of cells that move parts of the body
pores	tiny holes in the skin that let out sweat
saliva	the liquid in the mouth that helps people swallow food
sweat	the salty liquid that comes out of skin pores when people are hot

Explain the purpose of a glossary—to provide the meanings of words that a reader may not know. Point out that when we read non-fiction books aloud, we do not read the glossary. Ask students to tell what cells are.

Explain that the purpose of an index is to tell where information can be found in a book. Ask students which pages have information about sweat (pages 5 and 23).

Index

Bacteria 10–11, 21, 23	Nails 18–19
Doctors 20	Pores 5, 23
Ears 14–15	Saliva 9, 23
Eyelashes 13	Skin 4–7, 16
Eyes 12–13	Sweat 5, 23
Hair 6, 13, 16–17, 18	Taste buds 8
Microscope 3, 20, 22, 23	Tongue 8
Mouth 9, 10, 11	
Muscles 6, 12, 23	

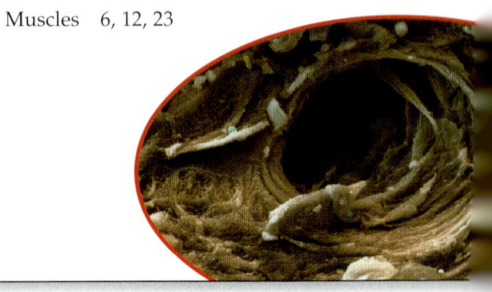

■ **Text Comprehension**

Ask *What is the most important idea of this book?* (Cells make up the different parts of the body.)

Ask *Which parts of the body are made of dead cells?* (the top layer of skin, nails, hair)

Ask *What do cells in the blood do?* (They keep the cells in the rest of the body healthy, and they fight bacteria and other germs.)

Ask *What do doctors use to look at cells?* (a microscope)

Chapter 1 Your Skin

Your skin is made of old and new cells. The top of your skin is made of old, dead cells. Every day, you lose lots and lots of these cells. New skin cells grow under the old cells.

Your skin helps to keep you cool. Skin has tiny holes called pores. Every time you get hot, drops of sweat come out of each pore. The sweat dries on your skin. It helps you feel cool.

If you feel cold or something scares you, you get goosebumps on your skin. You get goosebumps when tiny muscles under your skin pull the roots of your hairs. Each hair then stands up.

The skin on your hands and feet is thick. This thick skin is made up of lots of little bumps. The bumps help your hands and feet to grip things.

Chapter 2 Your Mouth

Your tongue has lots of tiny bumps, too. Some of these bumps have cells called taste buds. Taste buds tell you if something is sweet, sour, or salty.

■ Fluency Flip Page

The **Fluency Flip Page** of the **Student Book** contains a passage from the book to facilitate timed reading. For more information on timed reading and other ways of assessing fluency, see the **Teacher's Lesson Folder**.